COPYRIGHT

Copyright © 2024 by Sage Everest

All rights reserved. No part of this book may be reproduced, distributed, or transmitted in any form or by any means, including photocopying, recording, or other electronic or mechanical methods, without the prior written permission of the author, except in the case of brief quotations embodied in critical reviews and specific other non-commercial uses permitted by copyright law. For permission requests, please contact the publisher at the address below.

This book is a work of personal development and inspiration. The stories, insights, and suggestions are intended to offer support and motivation, but readers should seek appropriate professional advice when needed. The author and publisher disclaim any liability concerning the use of this information.

First Edition

FINANCIAL HABITS:

Building Wealth One Habit at a Time

Part 1: Understanding Your Financial Behavior
- **Chapter 1: The Psychology of Money**
    - Discuss common psychological barriers to effective money management.
    - Introduce the idea of mindset shifts for financial success.
- **Chapter 2: The Habit Loop in Finance**
    - Explain the cue-routine-reward loop in the context of financial habits.
    - How to identify triggers of poor financial decisions.

Part 2: Core Financial Habits
- **Chapter 3: Habit 1 - Tracking Your Spending**
    - Practical steps to make it evident and straightforward.
    - Tools and apps to assist in financial tracking.
- **Chapter 4: Habit 2 - Budgeting Wisely**
    - Make it attractive: gamifying budgeting.
    - Setting short-term and long-term financial goals.
- **Chapter 5: Habit 3 - Saving Consistently**
    - Make it satisfying: reward systems for reaching savings goals.
    - Techniques to automate saving and make it foolproof.

Part 3: Advanced Financial Habits

- **Chapter 6: Habit 4 - Investing Regularly**
    - Understanding basic investment principles.
    - Setting up a simple, repeatable investing routine.
- **Chapter 7: Habit 5 - Managing Debt**
    - Strategies to reduce and eliminate debt.
    - How to prioritize different types of debt.
- **Chapter 8: Habit 6 - Increasing Your Income**
    - Ideas and habits for side hustles and increasing main income streams.
    - Networking and professional development as customary practices.

Part 4: Overcoming Challenges and Setbacks
- **Chapter 9: Adapting to Financial Changes**
    - How to modify your financial habits when life changes (e.g., marriage, children, retirement).
    - Case studies on adapting financial plans during crises.
- **Chapter 10: Creating a Financially Healthy Lifestyle**
    - Integrating all habits into a cohesive lifestyle.
    - Long-term maintenance strategies.

INTRODUCTION: THE POWER OF FINANCIAL HABITS

If you've ever tried to manage your money better—by saving more, paying off debt, or investing smarter—you've probably experienced the frustration of falling back into old patterns. You set goals and make plans, and yet, somehow, the progress never sticks. Sound familiar? You're not alone.

Here's the good news: The key to transforming your financial life isn't about making drastic changes or cutting out every little indulgence. It's about building small, sustainable habits that move the needle daily. Tiny, consistent steps that, over time, lead to significant financial gains. The kind of change that sticks.

I used to believe that financial success came from mastering complex strategies, finding the perfect investment, or landing a high-paying job. But after years of trial and error (and some hard lessons along the way), I realized that real change comes from the habits we form around money—those daily decisions that seem insignificant but compound over time.

In this book, we will explain how you can take control of your financial life by focusing on habits—not significant, sweeping changes, but small, simple actions that you can incorporate into your daily routine. Whether you're trying to save for a big purchase, reduce debt, or build long-term wealth, mastering your financial habits is the key to reaching your goals.

Why Habits Matter in Finance

Most of our financial behaviors are automatic. Think about it—how often do you consider the decision to grab a coffee on the way to work, to buy that new gadget online, or to wait until the last minute to pay a bill? These choices are often driven by habits—unconscious routines we've built over time.

And here's the kicker: These small, seemingly trivial habits shape your financial reality. A daily $5 coffee might not feel like a big deal, but over a year, that adds up to over $1,800. Imagine if you redirected just a portion of that money into a savings account or an investment. The compound effect over time would be significant.

I'm not saying you must give up your coffee runs or live a life of extreme frugality. How you handle your money daily and your small decisions are the foundation of financial success. The great thing about habits is that once you build them, they run on autopilot. They become effortless. And the results start to stack up without you having to make enormous sacrifices constantly.

HOW SMALL HABITS CHANGED MY FINANCIAL LIFE

Let me take you back to when I started earning a steady paycheck. I was fresh out of school, excited about my new job, and eager to enjoy my hard-earned money. Every payday, I'd reward myself with a fancy dinner or a new gadget. It felt great—at first. But by the end of each month, I was always scrambling to make ends meet.

It wasn't that I didn't make enough money. I didn't have a system. My spending habits were out of control because I had no actual habits to help me manage my money. I'd spend impulsively and save whatever was left—usually not much. I told myself I'd figure it out next month. But "next month" always looked the same as the last.

I needed a change. And that change came not from some complicated financial plan but from a simple decision: I started automating my savings. Every payday, before I could even touch my money, a percentage was automatically transferred to my savings account. I didn't have to think about it. The habit was in place, and suddenly, I was saving consistently without effort. The reward? Watching my savings grow.

WHAT TO EXPECT IN THIS BOOK

Over the following chapters, you'll learn how to apply these six principles to your financial life. I'll walk you through how to build sustainable habits tailored to your unique situation. You'll also hear real-life stories, practical advice, and actionable steps you can use today.

By the end of this book, you'll have a clear roadmap for building wealth, reducing financial stress, and gaining control of your money—not through drastic changes but through small, intentional habits that you can rely on for years to come.

This journey isn't about being perfect with money. It's about making progress, one habit at a time.

Let's get started.

PART 1: UNDERSTANDING YOUR FINANCIAL BEHAVIOR

Part 1 explores how your mindset and habits influence your financial decisions. By understanding the psychological and emotional factors that shape how you handle money, you can gain valuable insights into your spending, saving, and investing behaviors. This section also breaks down the patterns behind financial habits, helping you identify triggers and routines that may hold you back. With this knowledge, you'll be equipped to rewire your habits and make more intelligent, consistent financial choices for long-term success.

CHAPTER 1: THE PSYCHOLOGY OF FINANCIAL HABITS

Introduction: The Power of Small Financial Changes

When managing money, most focus on big goals—buying a home, paying off debt, or saving for retirement. But what if the key to reaching those financial milestones wasn't about making dramatic changes overnight? What if, instead, it was about making minor, incremental improvements every day? That's where financial habits come into play.

Think of your financial life like a large ship at sea. If you steer it just a few degrees to the left or right, you'll end up at a completely different destination over time. The same is true for your finances. Small changes in how you manage money today can lead to massive financial shifts in the future.

I didn't always understand this. When I started earning money, I believed that if I wanted to change my financial situation, I had to make drastic decisions—like cutting out all non-essential spending or throwing everything into savings. But I quickly found out that drastic measures are hard to sustain. That's when I learned the true power of financial habits. I could see real, lasting progress by making minor, manageable adjustments to my daily financial routines.

Understanding Habit Formation: Why Financial Behavior Matters

Habits are behaviors we repeat so often that they become automatic. Once formed, habits take very little mental energy to maintain—they're the brain's way of saving effort. And this is why habits can be your greatest ally or worst enemy when managing money.

The first step in changing your financial habits is recognizing that many daily money decisions are part of an unconscious routine. Have you ever found yourself buying something impulsively, only to wonder afterward why you even made the purchase? That's your brain running on autopilot, following the same pattern it's been trained to follow.

Understanding how habits form is the key to reshaping your financial life. Habits follow a simple loop: cue, routine, and reward. The **cue** triggers the behavior (e.g., seeing an email about a sale). The **routine** is the behavior (e.g., clicking "buy" without thinking). The **reward** is the positive feeling that follows (e.g., the thrill of purchasing something new).

By becoming aware of these loops, you can start to take control of them and reshape your financial habits. It's not about denying yourself or creating an unsustainable budget—it's about creating new, healthier habits that serve your long-term financial goals.

My First Encounter with Financial Habits

When I received my first paycheck, I was ecstatic. When the money hit my account, I immediately planned how to spend it. The cue was my paycheck notification; the routine was spending it on things I didn't need, and the reward was the temporary happiness I felt after buying new clothes, gadgets, or eating out. But soon enough, I realized that I had nothing left by the end of the month, and saving felt impossible.

This pattern repeated itself for months until I decided I needed to change. Instead of splurging after getting paid, I immediately set aside a small percentage of my income for savings. The new cue was receiving my paycheck, the routine was automating a transfer to my savings account, and the reward was watching my savings grow. Over time, this small change became a habit, and I barely noticed the money I wasn't spending. What I did notice, however, was how much more secure I felt as my savings grew.

Family Story: My Mother's Approach to Budgeting

Growing up, I witnessed my mother's disciplined approach to budgeting. Every payday, she would divide her income into categories: bills, groceries, savings, and a small amount for discretionary spending. This was her routine, and she stuck to it diligently. Her cue was receiving her paycheck, her routine was setting up her monthly budget, and her reward was the peace of mind from knowing her financial obligations were covered and she was steadily saving for the future.

At the time, I didn't understand why she was so organized. But as I got older and began managing my money, I realized that her system wasn't about restriction but freedom. By creating healthy financial habits, she didn't have to worry about unexpected expenses or falling behind on bills. She had built a financial cushion, giving her the flexibility to enjoy life without stress.

The Six Laws of Behavior Change and Financial Habits

Now that you understand the importance of financial habits, let's explore how to change them. We can apply six principles to ensure these habits stick and become part of your daily financial routine.

1. Make it Obvious

The first step in changing your financial habits is to make them noticeable. You must bring your current habits into the light to improve your financial situation. One way to do this is by tracking your spending. Most people do not know where their money goes each month because their financial habits are hidden. By writing down every expense or using a budgeting app, you make your financial behavior visible and, more importantly, manageable.

The first time I started tracking my spending, I was shocked by how much I spent on things I didn't even think about—like daily coffee runs or small impulse buys online. Making these expenses obvious was the first step toward changing my financial behavior.

2. Make it Attractive

If you want to stick to a financial habit, you must make it attractive. Let's face it—saving money isn't always as fun as spending it, so how do you motivate yourself to save and spend less? You can pair your financial habits with something enjoyable.

For example, I used to dread sitting down to review my budget. It felt like a chore. But then I turned it into a routine I could look forward to. I brewed my favorite coffee, played some relaxing music, and made it quiet and enjoyable. Suddenly, budgeting wasn't something I avoided—it was something I began to enjoy.

Another way to make saving attractive is to set short-term goals with rewards. For instance, if you save $100 monthly for six months, reward yourself with something special—a small purchase or a night out. This creates a positive association with saving.

3. Make it Easy

One of the biggest reasons people fail to stick to financial habits is that they complicate things. The more steps involved, the harder it is to maintain the habit. That's why saving and managing your money quickly is essential.

One of the easiest ways to do this is through automation. Set up automatic transfers to your savings account as soon as you get paid. This way, the decision to save is made for you, and you don't have to rely on willpower to put money aside. Automating your finances removes friction and ensures that you're consistently building good financial habits without extra effort.

4. Make it Satisfying

Humans are wired to seek instant gratification, so long-term financial goals like retirement or paying off debt can be challenging. The key to sticking with these habits is to make them immediately satisfying.

While the ultimate reward of financial success may be years away, you can create smaller rewards to motivate yourself. For example, if you stick to your weekly budget, treat yourself to something small—a favorite meal or a relaxing evening. These small rewards help reinforce the habit and make the process enjoyable, even when the bigger goal feels far off.

5. Make it Social

Humans are social creatures, and we tend to adopt the habits of those around us. If you want to change your financial habits, consider involving others. Find a group of friends or family members who also want to improve their financial health and hold each other accountable.

One year, a close friend and I started a savings challenge. We set individual goals and checked in with each other every week. Knowing someone else was working toward similar goals kept me motivated and on track. Making financial habits social creates a support system that helps you stay committed.

6. Make it Reflective

The final law is reflection. Regularly reviewing your financial habits and progress is essential to staying on course. Set aside time every month or quarter to assess where you stand financially. Are your savings growing? Are you staying within your budget? Do you need to adjust your goals?

I started doing this quarterly, and it made a huge difference. By reflecting on my financial habits, I could identify what was working and what needed improvement. It also allowed me to celebrate my progress, which motivated me to keep going.

ACTIONABLE STEPS: HOW TO START CHANGING YOUR FINANCIAL HABITS TODAY

Now that we've covered the six laws of behavior change and how they apply to financial habits, it's time to implement these ideas. The key is to start small and build momentum. Here are three simple, actionable steps you can begin today:

1. **Track Every Expense for a Week**
    - For the next seven days, write down or log everything you spend money on. This will help you make your financial habits **obvious**. List it, whether it's a $2 coffee or your grocery bill. Review your list at the end of the week and identify areas where you can improve. This is the first step toward becoming aware of where your money goes.
2. **Set Up Automatic Savings**
    - If you haven't already, automatically transfer your checking account to your savings account. Make it **easy** by automating the process—this removes the need for daily decisions and

ensures you're saving regularly. Start with a manageable amount, even if it's just $50 or $100 per month. As the habit sticks, you can increase this amount.

3. **Join a Financial Accountability Group**
    - Find a friend or family member who shares your financial goals and create a support system. This makes your financial habits **social**, and the accountability will motivate you to stay on track. You could also join an online group focused on savings challenges or budgeting—anywhere others can support you in building these habits.

CONCLUSION: SMALL CHANGES, BIG RESULTS

Changing your financial habits isn't about making drastic decisions or transforming your financial situation overnight. Instead, it's about making small, manageable changes you can sustain over the long term. You can reshape how you handle money by following the six laws—making your financial habits obvious, attractive, easy, satisfying, social, and reflective.

These small habits, like tracking your expenses, automating savings, and seeking support from others, may initially seem insignificant. But over time, they add up. Each new habit you create strengthens your financial foundation, bringing you closer to your goals, whether buying a house, paying off debt, or retiring comfortably.

The journey to financial success is a marathon, not a sprint. And the good news is you don't have to make significant changes simultaneously. You can start small—one habit at a time. The most important thing is to begin today, and with the framework provided by the six laws of behavior change, you're well-equipped to succeed.

CHAPTER 2: THE HABIT LOOP IN FINANCE

Have you ever spent money without thinking and wondered, *"Why did I even buy that?"* Or maybe you've noticed that you never quite save as much as you plan, but you're unsure where your money went. The truth is that much of our financial behavior is driven by habits—automatic routines we fall into without realizing it. This is where the **habit loop** comes in.

Understanding how the **habit loop** works is critical to transforming your financial habits. At its core, every habit operates on a loop: **cue**, **routine**, and **reward**. This loop explains how we fall into good and bad habits and, more importantly, how to change them.

The Habit Loop: Cue, Routine, Reward

Let's break it down.

- **Cue**: The cue is the trigger that starts the habit. It could be anything—an emotion, a situation, or even a specific time of day. In financial terms, a cue might be seeing a paycheck hit your account, receiving an email about a sale, or simply feeling bored or stressed.
- **Routine**: The routine is the behavior or action you perform in response to the cue. If the cue is seeing a paycheck in your bank account, the routine might be immediately spending some of that money on a purchase you've been eyeing. If the cue is boredom, the routine might be scrolling through an online store and buying something you don't need.
- **Reward**: The reward is the positive reinforcement from

completing the routine. This could be the instant gratification of buying something new, the temporary relief from stress, or the fleeting sense of control over your finances. The reward reinforces the behavior, making you more likely to repeat the habit.

Together, the cue-routine-reward loop drives many of our financial decisions, often without us even being aware. But once you understand this loop, you can start to change it.

How Financial Habits Are Formed

Let me give you an example from my own life. For the longest time, my financial habits were utterly unconscious. Every time I got paid, I would feel a sense of excitement (the cue), and my immediate reaction was to spend some of that money (the routine). The reward? A quick hit of happiness from buying something new—whether it was a fancy meal, new clothes, or even gadgets I didn't need. This habit loop repeated itself every payday, and by the end of the month, I'd always wonder where my money went.

It wasn't until I learned about the habit loop that I realized my behavior wasn't random. I was following a predictable pattern. The problem was that the rewards I chased were temporary and weren't leading me to my long-term financial goals.

Once I identified the loop, I could begin to change it. Instead of spending impulsively after getting paid, I set up a new routine: automating a portion of my paycheck into a savings account. The reward? Watching my savings grow each month—a far more satisfying feeling than the temporary thrill of buying something I didn't need. The key to this transformation was becoming aware of the habit loop and reshaping it to serve my financial goals.

Identifying the Triggers of Poor Financial Decisions

So, how do you start identifying your financial habit loops, especially those holding you back? The first step is to **determine the cues**—the triggers that lead to poor financial decisions. These triggers often fall into a few common categories:

1. **Emotional Triggers**: Have you ever noticed that you spend more time feeling down, stressed, or anxious? Emotional spending is a standard financial habit loop. The cue might be a bad day at work or feeling overwhelmed by personal challenges. The routine is spending money—whether it's on food, clothes, or something to "treat yourself." The reward is temporary relief from the negative emotion, but it doesn't last, and the cycle repeats.

2. **Environmental Triggers**: Sometimes, your surroundings can cue financial habits without you even realizing it. For example, walking past a favorite store or browsing online shopping sites during downtime might trigger the habit of impulse buying. The cue is simply being in a situation where spending is easy, the routine is making a purchase, and the reward is the quick satisfaction of owning something new.

3. **Social Triggers**: We often spend money because of social pressure. When friends invite you to an expensive dinner or a shopping trip, it can be hard to say no. The cue is being with friends who are spending money, the routine is joining in, and the reward is fitting in or enjoying the social experience.

4. **Situational Triggers**: These triggers are tied to specific events or moments, like payday, tax refunds, or seasonal sales. The cue is receiving extra money or seeing a limited-time offer; the routine is spending because it feels like the right time, and the reward is often the sense of "taking advantage" of a financial opportunity.

You can begin to disrupt the loop once you recognize these cues in your life.

How to Change the Habit Loop

The good news is that once you've identified the cues that trigger your financial habits, you can change the routine and, ultimately, the outcome. Here's how to begin:

1. **Identify the Cue**: The first step is determining what triggers your financial habit. Start by paying attention to your behavior throughout the week. When do you feel the urge to spend? Is it after checking your bank account? Is it when you're bored or stressed? Write down what you notice, and look for patterns.

2. **Interrupt the Routine**: Once you've identified the cue, the next step is interrupting the routine. Instead of immediately acting on the urge to spend, try delaying the purchase. Give yourself 24 hours before buying something you don't need. This slight pause can help break the automatic loop and give you time to reconsider the decision.

3. **Create a New Routine**: To change your financial habits, you must replace the old routine with a new one. For example, if your cue is stress, instead of turning to online shopping as a coping mechanism, try a healthier routine—like going for a walk, journaling, or calling a friend. If the cue is receiving a paycheck, set up an automatic transfer to savings before you even think about spending. The key is to swap out the behavior while keeping the cue the same.

4. **Find a Better Reward**: The final step in changing the habit loop is finding a reward that aligns with your financial goals. Instead of getting a quick dopamine hit from an impulsive purchase, focus on long-term rewards like growing your savings or reaching a financial milestone. You can also create smaller rewards to keep yourself motivated, like having a nice meal after hitting a savings goal or celebrating with a fun (and budget-friendly) activity.

Personal Story: Breaking the Online Shopping Habit

Let me tell you how I broke my habit of online shopping. Every evening after work, I would scroll through online stores to unwind. The cue was boredom; the routine was buying something small, and the reward was the temporary excitement of receiving a package a few days later. But over time, I realized that this habit was draining my finances, and the thrill of those purchases never lasted.

Once I recognized the habit loop, I decided to change it. The cue (boredom after work) was still there, but instead of shopping online, I replaced the routine. I started reading or going for a short walk to relax. The reward? Feeling more accomplished and saving money in the process. Over time, the urge to shop online faded, and I built a healthier routine aligned with my financial goals.

CONCLUSION: TAKE CONTROL OF YOUR FINANCIAL HABIT LOOPS

Financial habits follow a predictable loop of cues, routines, and rewards like all habits. By identifying the cues that trigger your poor financial decisions, interrupting the routines, and finding better rewards, you can break the cycle and create new habits that support your long-term financial goals.

The key to financial success isn't willpower or deprivation—it's about understanding the behaviors that drive your decisions and making small, intentional changes to those behaviors. The habit loop is a powerful tool that can help you take control of your finances, one decision at a time.

In the next chapter, we'll dive deeper into how you can make these changes stick by learning how to **make your financial habits attractive**—because if a habit isn't enjoyable, it's hard to keep it going.

Let's start taking control of those habit loops and transform your finances for the better.

PART 2: CORE FINANCIAL HABITS

This section will explore the fundamental financial habits that lay the foundation for long-term economic success. These habits, though simple in concept, are compelling when practiced consistently. By making these habits obvious, attractive, easy, and satisfying, you'll develop a system that takes the stress out of managing money and turns financial management into a routine you can enjoy and stick with for the long term.

CHAPTER 3: HABIT 1 – TRACKING YOUR SPENDING

If there's one financial habit that will change your outlook on money, it's this: **tracking your spending**. Without this foundational habit, it's impossible to truly understand where your money is going, let alone control it. Tracking every expense might sound tedious, but here's the truth: when you make your spending obvious, you gain the power to direct your financial life with intention.

Most people have no idea where their money goes. You get your paycheck, you pay your bills, and somehow, there's less money left than you expected by the end of the month. Where did it all go? The first step to taking control of your financial future is understanding exactly where your money is going—down to the last cent.

This chapter will explain why tracking your spending is essential, how to do it sustainably and efficiently, and why making this habit attractive and satisfying will help you stick to it long-term.

Why Tracking Your Spending Is So Important

Think of your finances like a fitness journey. If you want to lose weight or get fit, any trainer would first tell you to track what you're eating and how much you're exercising. How can you progress if you don't know what's going into your body or how much energy you're burning?

The same principle applies to your money. Without tracking your spending, your finances are running on autopilot. You do not know how much goes toward essentials like rent and groceries versus how much is wasted on things you don't even remember buying. Tracking brings visibility. It shines a light on hidden patterns that may be draining your bank account without you even realizing it.

When you track your spending, it's like hitting the pause button on your financial habits. You can step back, see the whole picture, and make informed decisions. Suddenly, you're no longer wondering where your money went—you're telling it where to go.

The Power of Awareness: How Small Expenses Add Up

When I started tracking my spending, I was shocked at how the little things added up. You know how it goes: a coffee here, lunch out there, a quick online purchase, and before you know it, you've spent hundreds of dollars on things you didn't plan for.

Let's take the famous example of the **Latte Factor**. It's a term to describe how spending a small amount of money regularly—like $5 on a latte daily—can add up to a significant sum over time. At first glance, $5 doesn't seem like much. But let's break it down:

- $5 a day is $35 a week.
- That's $150 a month.
- over a year, that's $1,800.

Imagine what you could do with an extra $1,800 yearly. Maybe that's the start of an emergency fund, the additional payments you need to pay off debt faster, or even a vacation fund. Tracking your spending allows you to see these patterns and, more importantly, gives you the power to change them.

But tracking your spending isn't about depriving yourself. It's about making conscious choices. Once you know where your money is going, you can decide if that $5 latte is worth it or if you'd redirect it toward something else that brings you more value.

Making Tracking Obvious and Easy

What is the biggest reason people don't track their spending? It seems complicated or overwhelming. But the key to building any habit—especially one that has the potential to change your financial future—is to make it **evident** and **straightforward**.

Here's how you can do that:

1. **Choose a Tracking Method You'll Stick With**: You don't need to track your spending in a fancy way—just in a way that works for you. Some people love using a simple notebook and pen. Others prefer using a spreadsheet. And many people swear by apps that automate the process for them.
    - If you like a hands-on approach, grab a notebook or use a simple Excel spreadsheet to log every purchase. Divide your expenses into housing, groceries, entertainment, and discretionary spending categories.
    - If you prefer automation, try using an app like **Mint**, **YNAB (You Need a Budget)**, or **PocketGuard**. These apps sync with your bank accounts and credit cards, automatically categorize your spending, and clearly show where your money is going in real-time.
2. **Make It Visible**: Keep your spending log visible and accessible. If you're using a notebook or a spreadsheet, set it on your desk or kitchen counter so you'll see it daily. If you're using an app, set reminders on your phone to check in on your spending daily or weekly. The more you interact with your tracking system, the more likely you will stick with it.
3. **Start Small**: If you've never tracked your spending before, don't try to track every penny immediately—it can feel overwhelming. Start by monitoring your most

significant or frequent expenses, like groceries, dining out, and subscriptions. Once you get comfortable, you can start tracking smaller purchases as well.

Tools and Apps to Assist in Financial Tracking

Let's talk about the tools and apps that can make tracking your spending almost effortless. One of the best things about living in the digital age is that technology can handle the heavy lifting. If you're not into manually recording every purchase, these tools will become your new best friend.

1. **Mint**: Mint is a free budgeting app that links to your bank, credit card, and investment accounts. It automatically categorizes your purchases, tracks your spending in real-time, and offers a complete picture of your financial health. You can also set custom spending goals and get alerts if you approach your limits in a particular category.

2. **YNAB (You Need a Budget)**: YNAB is perfect if you prefer a more proactive approach to budgeting and tracking. Unlike Mint, which focuses on categorizing past purchases, YNAB encourages you to assign every dollar you earn to a specific purpose (such as bills, savings, or discretionary spending) before you spend it. It's beneficial if you're trying to stick to a budget and need a tool to keep you accountable.

3. **PocketGuard**: If you need to know precisely how much money you can spend at any moment, PocketGuard is for you. It's designed to help you avoid overspending by showing how much "pocket money" you have left after accounting for bills, goals, and necessities. This is great for people who struggle with impulse purchases or overspend without realizing it.

4. **Good Old Pen and Paper**: Don't underestimate the power of a simple notebook and pen. There's something

satisfying about manually writing down your purchases and physically seeing your spending habits on paper. If you're more tactile, try carrying a small notebook to jot down every purchase.

Turning Tracking into a Habit

Now that you understand why tracking your spending is essential and how to make it easy, the next step is turning this into a habit. Habits form when you repeat a behavior enough times that it becomes automatic. The goal is tracking your spending to become second nature—something you do without thinking.

Here's how to build this habit:

1. **Pair It with an Existing Habit**: The easiest way to build a new habit is to attach it to something you already do. For example, if you always check your phone in the morning, use that time to log into your spending app and review your purchases. If you're more of a night owl, you can log your expenses right before bed.
2. **Reward Yourself**: Give yourself a small reward every time you successfully track your spending for a week. This could be treating yourself to an excellent coffee or a relaxing evening. The key is to make the habit feel satisfying so you'll want to continue doing it.
3. **Stay Consistent**: Habits take time to form. Aim to track your spending consistently for at least 30 days. By the end of the month, it will start to feel like a regular part of your routine.

The Long-Term Benefits of Tracking Your Spending

The benefits of tracking your spending extend far beyond the short-term satisfaction of knowing where your money is going. Over time, this habit gives you the power to make better financial decisions, save more, and feel more in control of your money.

When you consistently track your spending, you'll be able to:

- **Identify spending patterns**: You'll start to notice trends, like how much you spend on groceries or how much those small online purchases add up. This awareness allows you to make intentional decisions about where to cut back or where to reallocate funds.
- **Create better budgets**: With accurate data on your spending, you can create a budget that works. No more guessing how much you spend on dining out or utilities—you'll know the numbers and be able to plan accordingly.
- **Reach financial goals faster**: Whether saving for a vacation, paying off debt, or building an emergency fund, tracking your spending gives you the insight to hit your goals faster. You'll see where you can save, and you'll be able to adjust your spending to prioritize your goals.

CONCLUSION: START TRACKING TODAY

Tracking your spending is the first step toward fully controlling your finances. It doesn't have to be complicated or overwhelming. By making the process obvious, easy, and fun, you can build a habit that will transform how you manage money.

Remember, you can't improve what you don't measure. Start today, and watch how much more intentional, empowered, and in control you feel over your financial life.

CHAPTER 4: HABIT 2 – BUDGETING WISELY

Budgeting—just the word can make you feel restricted or even a little overwhelmed. But here's the truth: budgeting isn't about saying "no" to everything you enjoy. It's about saying "yes" to the things that matter. When you budget wisely, you create a roadmap for your financial life. You're not guessing where your money goes anymore—you're telling it where to go.

Most people avoid budgeting because they think it's restrictive or boring. However, when done correctly, budgeting becomes empowering. It gives you control, allowing you to prioritize your money in a way that supports your goals and values. In this chapter, we'll explore how to turn budgeting into an engaging, enjoyable habit by making it **attractive** and how to use simple strategies to ensure you're budgeting wisely for both the short and long term.

Reframing Budgeting: Why It's Not About Deprivation

Before we dive into the "how," let's tackle the biggest misconception about budgeting: that it's about cutting out everything fun or depriving yourself of life's little pleasures. In reality, a reasonable budget is the opposite. It's not about limiting what you can do with your money but maximizing it.

Think of your budget as a **spending plan**. It's a tool to help you do more with your money—whether saving for a big vacation, paying off debt, or just having the freedom to buy the things you enjoy without guilt. Instead of asking, "How little can I spend?" ask,

"How can I spend smarter to get more value?"

Step 1: Setting the Foundation – Know Your Income and Expenses

To build a successful budget, it would be best to start by clearly understanding your financial picture. That means knowing exactly how much you bring in each month and how much you spend.

1. **Calculate Your Income**: Start by listing all your sources of income. This includes your salary, side gigs, rental income, or other earnings. Knowing your monthly income gives you the foundation for what you have available to work with.

2. **Track Your Expenses**: Chapter 3 discussed the importance of spending tracking. Once you've tracked your spending for at least a month, you'll have a clear idea of where your money is going. Now, categorize your expenses into essential and non-essential categories. Essentials might include housing, utilities, groceries, and transportation, while non-essentials include dining out, entertainment, and hobbies.

Step 2: Making Budgeting Attractive – Gamify Your Budget

Budgeting doesn't have to feel like a chore. One of the best ways to stick with your budget is to make it fun. **Gamifying** your budget can transform the process from restrictive to rewarding.

Here are some ways to make budgeting more engaging:

- **Set Weekly Challenges**: Challenge yourself to save an extra $20 this week by cooking at home instead of eating out. Or, see if you can spend $50 less than usual on entertainment. Each time you hit your target, give yourself a small reward—a coffee, a movie night, or the satisfaction of knowing you hit your goal.
- **Create a Budgeting Tracker**: Use a visual tracker to measure your progress. You could create a chart that

shows how much you've saved toward a specific goal, like a vacation or a new purchase. Every time you add to your savings, color in a chart section. This visual progress can be incredibly motivating, especially when you see how quickly your savings are growing.

- **Use a Budgeting App**: Apps like **YNAB** (You Need A Budget) or **EveryDollar** help you create a budget and stick to it by making the process interactive. Many apps allow you to categorize your spending, set savings goals, and track your progress in real time. Plus, they often come with features like notifications that alert you when you're approaching your spending limits.

- **Celebrate Wins**: Reward yourself each time you stay under budget in a particular category. This could be a simple treat like a favorite dessert or a special night out. Celebrating small wins along the way is essential to reinforce the habit.

Step 3: Creating a Budget That Works for You

Budgeting isn't one-size-fits-all. The key to budgeting wisely is creating a system that fits your life, goals, and values. Here's how to make a budget that feels empowering rather than restrictive:

1. **Start with the Essentials**: Once you've categorized your expenses, allocate a portion of your income to cover your essential costs first. These are your non-negotiables, like rent or mortgage payments, utilities, groceries, and transportation. Make sure these are fully covered before moving on to discretionary spending.

2. **Prioritize Your Goals**: Direct a portion of your income toward your financial goals after covering your essentials. This could be saving for an emergency fund, paying off debt, or contributing to retirement. Prioritize these goals before spending on non-essentials.
   - If you don't have an emergency fund, set aside $500 to $1,000 for unexpected expenses. Once that's in place, save 3 to 6 months' living expenses.

- If you have high-interest debt, prioritize paying it down aggressively. After covering your essentials, redirect any leftover funds toward making extra payments on your debt.
- If you're saving for retirement, ensure you're contributing to employer-sponsored retirement plans, especially if your employer offers a match. Free money? Yes, please!

3. **Allocate Non-Essential Spending**: Once your essentials and goals are covered, allocate the rest of your income to discretionary spending. You can decide how much to spend on dining out, entertainment, hobbies, and travel. The beauty of budgeting is that it allows you to devote yourself to it guilt-free because you know you've already taken care of your priorities.

Step 4: Setting Short-Term and Long-Term Goals

A reasonable budget doesn't just focus on the present—it balances your short-term and long-term financial goals. Here's how to approach both:

- **Short-Term Goals**: These are goals you can achieve within a year. Examples might include saving for a vacation, building an emergency fund, or paying off a credit card. Short-term goals are motivating because they offer quick wins. Break these goals into smaller milestones and track your progress along the way.

For example, if you're saving $1,200 for a vacation in 12 months, that's just $100 a month. Track it visually and celebrate each time you hit a milestone.

- **Long-Term Goals**: Long-term goals require more patience but are essential for financial security. These could include retirement savings, home buying, or investing wealth. The key to reaching long-term goals is consistency. Make saving for these goals automatic—set up automatic transfers to your savings or retirement accounts so that you're contributing consistently without thinking about it.

Real-Life Example: How Budgeting Helped Me Pay Off Debt

I was in credit card debt a few years ago, which seemed impossible. I made the minimum payments, but the balance wasn't shrinking fast enough. It wasn't until I created a budget that prioritized debt repayment that I finally started to make progress.

I gamified my debt repayment by setting small challenges for myself, like finding ways to cut back on unnecessary expenses so I could make extra credit card payments. Every time I hit a milestone, like paying off a $500 chunk of debt, I rewarded myself with something minor, like a dinner out. Over time, those small victories added up, and I was able to pay off the debt faster than I thought possible.

The most important lesson I learned was that budgeting doesn't mean deprivation—it means empowerment. Instead of feeling like I couldn't spend, I felt in control of where my money was going.

Step 5: Review and Adjust Regularly

Your budget isn't set in stone. Life changes, and so do your financial needs. Maybe you got a raise, your rent increased, or you've decided to save for something new. That's why it's essential to **review your budget regularly**—at least once a month—and adjust it as needed.

If you notice consistently overspending in a particular category, ask yourself why. Are your goals realistic, or do they need to be tweaked? The more you interact with your budget and make it a living document, the more likely you will stick with it.

CONCLUSION: BUDGETING AS A PATH TO FREEDOM

Budgeting is not about restricting yourself; it's about creating freedom. When you budget wisely, you're not stressed about overspending or where your money went. You know exactly how much you can spend on things that matter to you while still working toward your financial goals.

By making budgeting attractive through gamification, setting realistic short- and long-term goals, and reviewing your progress regularly, you'll find that budgeting becomes less of a chore and more of an empowering tool. Stick with it, and you'll see how small, intentional changes in how you allocate your money can significantly improve your financial life.

Next, we'll dive into **saving consistently**, the cornerstone of financial stability. Let's build on this budgeting foundation to ensure that your money isn't just spent wisely but saved with purpose.

CHAPTER 5: HABIT 3 – SAVING CONSISTENTLY

If there's one financial habit that can make or break your future, it's **saving consistently**. Saving isn't just about putting money away for a rainy day; it's about creating a cushion that allows you to achieve your goals, weather unexpected events, and build the life you want. The problem is, for many of us, saving can feel like an afterthought. We think, "I'll save whatever's left over after I spend," but often, nothing is left.

The secret to saving consistently lies in turning it from something you have to force yourself to do into something you do automatically—and even enjoy. This chapter will show you how to make saving a regular, painless part of your financial routine by leveraging the power of automation and reward systems. We'll also explore why saving doesn't have to feel like a sacrifice but can feel intensely satisfying.

Why Saving Consistently Is the Foundation of Financial Security

Imagine this: your car breaks down unexpectedly, or you lose your job. These things happen to everyone at some point, and when they do, your savings can be the difference between a financial crisis and a minor inconvenience.

But savings aren't just for emergencies. Consistent saving is also the gateway to achieving your dreams—buying a house, starting a business, or retiring comfortably. Every financial goal you set for yourself, big or small, requires saving. The problem most people face isn't a lack of income; it's a lack of systems for saving that income consistently.

Saving shouldn't be something you do once in a while or only when there's extra money. It needs to become an automatic part of managing your finances, like paying your bills. When you build a habit of saving consistently, you stop relying on willpower and start relying on systems. And that's where the magic happens.

Step 1: Automate Your Savings – Make It Easy

The most effective way to save consistently is to take willpower out of the equation entirely by automating your savings. Here's how it works: you set up an automatic transfer from your checking account to your savings account, and every time you get paid, a portion of your income is sent directly to savings without you having to lift a finger.

Why is this so powerful? Because it eliminates the temptation to spend that money. When you automate your savings, you never even see the money in your checking account, so you don't have to choose to save it—it's already done for you.

Here's how to do it:

1. **Set up automatic transfers**: Most banks allow you to set up recurring transfers from your checking account to your savings account. Choose a comfortable amount—10%, 20%, or even just $50 of each paycheck. The key is consistency.

2. **Use direct deposit**: If your employer offers direct deposit, you can deposit a portion of your paycheck directly into a savings account, bypassing your checking account entirely.

3. **Automate retirement savings**: If you can access a 401(k) or other retirement accounts, set up automatic contributions. Many employers even offer a matching

contribution, which is essentially free money, so make sure you're taking full advantage of that.

The beauty of automation is that it makes saving effortless. You don't have to think about it, debate whether you can afford it, or worry about forgetting. It's done.

Step 2: Make Saving Satisfying – Reward Systems for Reaching Goals

Saving money doesn't have to feel like a drag. One of the best ways to stay motivated to save is to create a **reward system**. The brain is wired to seek rewards, and giving ourselves small, satisfying incentives for hitting our savings goals reinforces the habit.

Here's how you can make saving satisfying:

- **Break big goals into smaller milestones**: If you're saving for something big—like a down payment on a house or a large emergency fund—break that goal into smaller chunks. For example, instead of focusing on saving $10,000, start by focusing on keeping the first $1,000.
- **Reward yourself for hitting milestones**: Give yourself a small reward every time you reach a savings milestone. This doesn't have to be expensive. It could be treating yourself to a dinner out, buying a book you've wanted, or spending a day doing something you love. The key is to create a positive association with saving so it feels rewarding rather than restrictive.
- **Visualize your progress**: Use a visual savings tracker—a chart, a graph, or even a physical jar you fill with money—to see how close you reach your goal. The act of seeing your progress builds momentum and makes you excited to keep saving.

Step 3: Automating for Short-Term and Long-Term Goals

When it comes to saving, one size does not fit all. You must consider your short-term and long-term financial goals and create a savings system that addresses both.

Short-Term Goals: You want to save for these in the next year or

two. Think of things like:
- An emergency fund (3 to 6 months of living expenses).
- A vacation.
- A new car.
- Home repairs.

For short-term goals, set up a separate savings account and automate transfers specifically for these purposes. It's helpful to label these accounts according to their purpose (most banks allow you to do this) so you know exactly what you're saving for.

Long-Term Goals: These are bigger goals that take several years—or even decades—to achieve, such as:
- Retirement.
- Buying a home.
- Starting a business.
- Funding your children's education.

For long-term goals, automation is even more critical. Set up automatic contributions to retirement accounts like 401(k), IRA, or investment accounts. By consistently contributing, you'll take advantage of compound interest, where your money grows faster because you're earning interest on both your original contributions and the already accumulated interest.

Step 4: Consistency Over Perfection

The thing about saving money is that it doesn't have to be perfect. You don't have to save a massive amount every month or beat yourself up if you miss a month or need to dip into your savings for something urgent. The key to financial success isn't perfection; it's consistency.

When you automate your savings and set clear goals, you create a system that works even when life gets busy. The magic of consistent saving is that even small amounts add up over time. It's not about saving $500 or $1,000 monthly. It's about saving $100 or $200 every month, month after month until you've built up enough to cover your goals.

A Personal Story: When I started saving, I felt overwhelmed by how much I wanted to save and how little progress I made. I set a goal of saving $10,000, but every time I looked at the goal, it felt impossible. So, I decided to break it down into smaller chunks. Instead of focusing on the entire $10,000, I aimed to save $500 every two months.

With automated transfers, I didn't even notice the money leaving my account, and before I knew it, I'd hit my first $500 milestone. Each time I reached a new milestone, I gave myself a small reward, like a nice dinner out or a new gadget I'd been eyeing. This kept me motivated and made the process enjoyable.

Step 5: Review and Adjust Your Savings Goals Regularly

As with budgeting, your savings goals will change over time. Maybe you've hit your goal of building an emergency fund, or you're saving more now because of a raise. That's why it's essential to **review your savings plan regularly**—at least every few months—and make adjustments as needed.

Ask yourself:
- Are you on track to hit your short-term and long-term goals?
- Can you increase your savings now that you're more comfortable with your budget?
- Do you need to adjust your automation for new financial priorities?

Reviewing your goals and adjusting your savings plan ensures you're always moving toward your financial targets, no matter how your life or circumstances change.

CONCLUSION: SAVING CONSISTENTLY IS THE KEY TO FINANCIAL FREEDOM

Consistent savings are the cornerstone of financial security and freedom. By automating your savings, satisfying the process with rewards, and balancing your short—and long-term goals, you'll build a financial cushion to handle life's surprises and confidently pursue your dreams.

Remember, it's not about perfection. It's about creating systems that work for you to save money without thinking about it. Every dollar saved is a step closer to financial freedom, and with the proper habits in place, saving can be both automatic and enjoyable.

Next, we'll discuss the final critical financial habit: investing, which involves turning your savings into long-term wealth.

PART 3: ADVANCED FINANCIAL HABITS

Once you've mastered the core financial habits—tracking your spending, budgeting wisely, and saving consistently—it's time to take your financial journey to the next level. This is where **investing regularly** comes in. Investing isn't just for the wealthy or financially savvy; it's a habit anyone can adopt to build long-term wealth and financial freedom.

CHAPTER 6: HABIT 4 – INVESTING REGULARLY

Investing can feel intimidating, especially if you've never done it before. Navigating the stock market, bonds, mutual funds, and various asset classes might seem like something only financial professionals can handle. But the truth is that **investing** doesn't have to be complicated. You don't need to be an expert to start, and you certainly don't need a fortune to invest. You need a simple, repeatable investing routine that you can follow consistently.

In this chapter, we'll break down the basics of investing, explore why it's essential for building wealth, and show you how to create a straightforward, automated investing plan that works for you.

Why Investing Is Key to Financial Freedom

Saving is significant, but saving alone won't make you wealthy. That's because the money you save in a bank account doesn't grow much over time, especially with low interest rates. Inflation—rising prices over time—means that your savings' purchasing power decreases if you're not earning a return on your money.

This is where **investing** comes in. When you invest, your money works for you. Instead of just sitting in a savings account, it grows. Thanks to **compound interest**, your investments can earn money over time—not just on your initial investment but on the earnings your investments generate. This snowball effect is how wealth is built.

To illustrate, imagine you invested $1,000 today at an annual return of 7% (the average long-term return of the stock market). In 30 years, that $1,000 would grow to approximately $7,600. Imagine you're contributing $100 a month to that same investment. Over 30 years, you'd have over $120,000 by investing regularly and letting compound interest work.

Understanding Basic Investment Principles

Before diving into setting up your investment routine, it's essential to understand some basic principles that guide how investing works. Knowing these concepts will help you make informed decisions and avoid common mistakes.

1. **The Power of Compound Interest**: This is the investing engine. Compound interest means you're earning interest not only on your initial investment but also on the returns your investment generates. Over time, this creates exponential growth, so the earlier you start investing, the more time your money has to grow.

2. **Risk vs. Reward**: All investments carry some level of risk, and typically, the greater the potential reward, the higher the risk. Stocks, for example, tend to offer higher returns over the long term but can be more volatile in the short term. Bonds, on the other hand, are generally safer but provide lower returns. The key to investing is finding a balance between risk and reward that aligns with your financial goals and comfort level.

3. **Diversification**: A common saying in investing is, "Don't put all your eggs in one basket." Diversification means spreading your money across different investments—such as stocks, bonds, and real estate—to reduce risk. When you diversify, a downturn in one area of the market won't have as significant an impact on your overall portfolio because other parts may be performing well.

4. **Time in the Market**: Trying to time the market—guessing when prices will go up or down—is a losing strategy for most people. Instead, the key to successful investing is **time in the market**. The longer you stay invested, the more likely you will benefit from the market's long-term growth.
5. **Dollar-Cost Averaging**: This simple strategy involves investing the same amount of money at regular intervals, regardless of whether the market is up or down. This reduces the risk of making poor investment decisions based on short-term market fluctuations and helps you build wealth consistently over time.

Setting Up a Simple, Repeatable Investing Routine

Now that you understand the basics let's discuss how to build a simple investing habit that you can stick to. Like saving, the key to investing regularly is to make it automatic and effortless.

Step 1: Determine How Much You Can Invest Regularly

Start by looking at your budget (from Chapter 4) to figure out how much you can comfortably invest each month. This doesn't need to be a considerable amount. Even if it's just $50 or $100 per month, the important thing is to get started and stay consistent. Over time, as your income grows or your financial situation improves, you can increase the amount you invest.

Step 2: Choose an Investment Account

The next step is to decide where to invest. Here are a few common types of accounts you might consider:

- **Employer-Sponsored Retirement Accounts (401(k), 403(b))**: If your employer offers a retirement plan like a 401(k), this is a great place to start, especially if they offer matching contributions. Contributing enough to get the full employer match is free, so take advantage of it.
- **Individual Retirement Accounts (IRAs)**: If you don't have access to a 401(k) or want to save more for

retirement, consider opening a Traditional or Roth IRA. These accounts offer tax benefits, which can help your investments grow more efficiently.
- **Taxable Investment Accounts**: If you've maxed out your retirement accounts or are saving for a goal unrelated to retirement (like buying a house), you can invest in a regular taxable brokerage account. There are no contribution limits; you can access your money anytime, but you'll have to pay taxes on your earnings.

Step 3: Automate Your Investments

Like automating your savings, automating your investments is the easiest way to stay consistent. Most investment platforms allow you to set up automatic contributions, so money is transferred from your checking account to your investment account at regular intervals—weekly, biweekly, or monthly.

By automating your investments, you eliminate the temptation to spend the money and ensure that you're investing consistently, no matter what the market does.

Step 4: Start with Low-Cost Index Funds or ETFs

For most people, the simplest and most effective way to invest is through low-cost **index funds** or **ETFs (Exchange-Traded Funds)**. These funds allow you to invest in a broad range of stocks or bonds, providing instant diversification. Index funds and ETFs are also much cheaper than actively managed funds, meaning more of your money is working for you.

Popular examples include:
- **Vanguard Total Stock Market Index Fund (VTSAX)**: A low-cost fund that tracks the entire U.S. stock market.
- **Vanguard S&P 500 ETF (VOO)**: A fund that tracks the 500 largest companies in the U.S., providing broad exposure to the market.

Investing in index funds or ETFs is a "set it and forget it" strategy. You don't have to worry about picking individual stocks or constantly monitoring the market—invest regularly and let your money grow over time.

Step 5: Review Your Investments Annually

Once you've set up your automated investing routine, it's essential to check in on your investments periodically—once a year is typically enough. During your annual review, ensure your portfolio aligns with your goals and adjust your contributions if necessary.

Avoid the temptation to check your investments too frequently, especially during market volatility. Remember, the goal is to stay invested for the long term.

Real-Life Example: How I Built an Investing Routine

When I started investing, I was overwhelmed by the options and didn't know where to begin. But I knew that if I waited until I felt "ready," I'd never start. So, I committed to investing $100 every month. I set up automatic contributions to a simple index fund, which was invested before I could spend it on something else.

At first, it didn't feel like much. $100 doesn't make a massive difference in a single month. But as the months went by, I saw my investment balance grow. The money I'd invested was now earning money on its own—thanks to compound interest. I didn't have to manage it or constantly check on it. By automating my investments, I could build wealth without the stress of trying to time the market.

Several years later, I've increased my contributions as my income has grown, and my initial $100 monthly contributions have multiplied into a sizable nest egg.

Conclusion: The Key to Building Wealth Is Consistency

Investing doesn't have to be complicated. The most successful investors often keep it simple and follow a consistent routine. By setting up a repeatable investing habit—whether it's contributing to your 401(k), IRA, or taxable account—you can harness the power of compound interest and build wealth over time.

The key is to start now, no matter how small. Even if you can only invest $50 or $100 a month, that money will grow over time, and as you gain confidence, you can increase your contributions. Remember, time in the market is more important than timing the market.

CHAPTER 7: HABIT 5 – MANAGING DEBT

Debt is a reality for most people at some point in their financial journey. Whether it's student loans, credit cards, car loans, or a mortgage, debt can feel overwhelming, but it doesn't have to control your life. **Managing debt wisely** is a critical financial habit that reduces stress and puts you on a path to financial freedom. When handled strategically, debt can even be a tool that helps you grow your wealth.

In this chapter, we'll explore practical strategies to reduce and eliminate debt, prioritize different types of debt, and manage debt to support your overall financial goals. The key to managing debt isn't just paying it off but doing so in a way that empowers you financially.

Understanding Debt: The Good, the Bad, and the Ugly

Not all debt is created equal. Some debt can be considered **"good debt,"** an investment in your future—like a mortgage or student loan—because it often comes with lower interest rates and is tied to appreciating assets or personal growth. **"Bad debt,"** on the other hand, typically involves high interest rates and is tied to depreciating assets or consumption, such as credit card debt or payday loans.

Before you can manage your debt effectively, you need to categorize it:

- **Good Debt**: Mortgages, student loans, business loans (if they help you generate income), and sometimes car loans (if needed for transportation).

- **Bad Debt**: Credit card balances, personal loans with high interest rates, and any debt used to fund discretionary spending like vacations or gadgets.

The first step in managing debt wisely is understanding how it impacts your financial picture.

Strategies to Reduce and Eliminate Debt

Once you know what kind of debt you're dealing with, it's time to implement strategies to reduce and eliminate it. Here are the two most effective methods for tackling debt:

1. **The Snowball Method**: The snowball method is about building momentum and staying motivated. With this strategy, you start by paying off your smallest debt first, regardless of the interest rate. Once that debt is paid off, you take the money you were putting toward it and apply it to the next smallest debt, and so on.

    The idea is to gain quick wins by eliminating smaller debts first, which gives you the psychological boost to keep going. Each time you pay off a debt, it frees up more money to tackle the next one, creating a snowball effect.

    Example: You have three debts:
    - $1,000 credit card balance at 18% interest
    - $5,000 car loan at 5% interest
    - $10,000 student loan at 4% interest

    Using the snowball method, you'd first focus on paying off the $1,000 credit card balance, regardless of the higher interest rate on other debts, because it's the smallest. Once that's paid off, you add the amount you were paying on the credit card to your car loan payments, accelerating the payoff process.

2. **The Avalanche Method**: The avalanche method focuses on paying off debt with the highest interest rate first, which can save you more money in the long run. Once the debt with the highest interest rate is paid off, you

move on to the next highest, and so on.

While this method is more efficient in saving on interest payments, it can take longer to see the psychological benefits, especially if your high-interest debt balances are large.

Example: Using the same debt from the previous example, with the avalanche method, you would start by paying off the credit card with 18% interest first, then move on to the car loan, and finally tackle the student loan. This method reduces the total amount of interest you pay over time.

How to Prioritize Different Types of Debt

It's not always easy to know where to start when you have multiple debts. Here's how you can prioritize them:

1. **Start with High-Interest Debt**: High-interest debt, especially credit card balances, should be a top priority because the interest can compound quickly, making it harder to pay down the balance over time.
2. **Consider Tax-Deductible Debt**: Some debts, like student loans or mortgages, offer tax advantages. These debts don't need to be paid off as aggressively, especially if they come with lower interest rates.
3. **Tackle Variable-Rate Debt Next**: If you have any loans with variable interest rates, it's essential to pay them off before interest rates rise, which can unexpectedly increase your monthly payments.
4. **Don't Forget About Small Balances**: If you have manageable small debts, don't be afraid to pay them off quickly, even if the interest rates aren't the highest. This will free up your mental space and finances to focus on more significant debts.

Creating a Debt Repayment Plan

A debt repayment plan is a roadmap that ensures you are paying down your debt in a structured and sustainable way. Here's how to create one:

1. **List All Your Debts**: Write down all your debts, including the balance, interest rate, and minimum payment for each. Include any loans, credit card balances, or personal debt.
2. **Choose Your Method**: Decide whether the snowball or avalanche method works better for your situation and personality. Some people are motivated by seeing quick wins, while others want to minimize the total interest paid.
3. **Make Extra Payments**: To accelerate the repayment process, make extra payments beyond the minimum. An additional $50 a month can make a big difference over time.
4. **Automate Payments**: Set up automatic payments to ensure you never miss a payment and to help avoid late fees. This also ensures that you stay consistent with your plan.
5. **Track Your Progress**: Track your debt repayment progress through a financial app or manually in a notebook or spreadsheet. Watching your debt decrease can be incredibly motivating.

Using Debt Strategically: When Debt Can Be a Tool

While the goal is to eliminate unnecessary debt, some can be used strategically to build wealth. For example, taking out a mortgage to buy a home can be a smart financial move if the property appreciates. Similarly, using a business loan to fund a venture that generates income can be considered an investment rather than a burden.

The key is to ensure that any debt you take on is calculated and that you plan to pay it off.

Real-Life Example: How I Paid Off $20,000 in Debt

In my twenties, I had $20,000 in debt, mostly from credit cards and student loans. At the time, it felt insurmountable, and I was paying hundreds of dollars a month just in interest. I knew I needed a plan.

I started by listing all of my debts, including their interest rates, balances, and minimum payments. After some research, I decided to follow the avalanche method because I had a very high-interest credit card that cost me a lot each month. I made minimum payments on my lower-interest debts while focusing all my extra income on paying off that credit card as fast as possible.

Every time I paid off a debt, I felt more in control of my finances. Slowly but surely, I worked through the rest of my debts, and within two years, I was debt-free. The freedom I felt afterward was incredible, and it taught me the value of having a clear plan and sticking to it.

CONCLUSION: TAKE CONTROL OF YOUR DEBT, DON'T LET IT CONTROL YOU

Debt can feel like a weight on your shoulders, but when managed wisely, it becomes manageable and even an opportunity for growth. By prioritizing high-interest debt, choosing the proper repayment method, and staying consistent, you can eliminate debt faster than you thought possible.

Remember, the goal isn't just to pay off debt; it's to do so in a way that supports your overall financial goals. Whether you choose the snowball method for quick wins or the avalanche method to save on interest, the most important thing is to start. With a solid plan, you'll be debt-free and ready to build lasting financial security.

Next, we'll explore how to **increase your income**—because reducing debt is just one side of the equation. Earning more allows you to save, invest, and reach your financial goals even faster.

CHAPTER 8: HABIT 6 – INCREASING YOUR INCOME

Managing your finances effectively isn't just about cutting expenses or eliminating debt—it's also about **growing your income**. While frugality and budgeting are essential, there's a limit to how much you can save. However, there's virtually no limit to how much you can earn. By continuously increasing your income, you can accelerate your financial goals and create a more prosperous future.

In this chapter, we'll explore ways to increase your income, whether through negotiating a raise, starting a side hustle, or investing in skills that boost your earning potential. We'll also discuss why increasing your income should be crucial to your financial strategy.

Why Increasing Your Income is a Game Changer

Increasing your income is one of the most potent ways to fast-track your financial success. While managing your money wisely is essential, having more money coming in gives you far more flexibility. It allows you to pay off debt faster, save more aggressively, and invest for the future.

Here's the thing: there's a limit to how much you can cut from your expenses, but there's no ceiling on how much you can earn. By focusing on growing your income, you unlock new opportunities for financial growth.

Here are a few reasons why increasing your income can be a game changer:
1. **Accelerates Debt Repayment**: With more income, you can make larger payments on your debt and eliminate it faster. The faster you pay off debt, the less you spend on interest.
2. **Boosts Savings and Investments**: Increasing your income allows you to contribute more to your savings and investments. This means your money will grow faster, thanks to the power of compound interest.
3. **Provides Financial Security**: Multiple income streams or higher salaries give you a safety net in financial emergencies. It also reduces your reliance on any one job or source of income.

Step 1: Negotiate a Raise at Work

One of the most straightforward ways to increase your income is to ask for a raise at your current job. You should be compensated if you deliver value, contribute to your company's success, and take on new responsibilities.

Here's how to successfully negotiate a raise:
1. **Do Your Research**: Before asking for a raise, research the average salary for your position in your industry. Websites like **Glassdoor** or **PayScale** can give you an idea of what people with similar experience and skills earn. Be sure to consider factors like location and years of experience.
2. **Prepare Your Case**: When asking for a raise, it is essential to be specific about why you deserve it. Keep a record of your accomplishments, contributions, and any new responsibilities you've taken on. Highlight how you've gone above and beyond and how your work has directly impacted the company's bottom line or success.
3. **Time It Right**: Timing is crucial when asking for a

raise. Consider the company's financial situation, the timing of performance reviews, and any recent wins or achievements you've had. You can increase your chances by asking for a raise after completing a significant project or contributing to the company's success.

4. **Be Confident and Professional**: When it comes time to negotiate, be confident in your worth. Approach the conversation professionally, emphasizing your value and contributions. Be prepared to discuss your research and explain why the raise is justified based on your performance and market rates.

Step 2: Start a Side Hustle

Starting a side hustle is a great option to increase your income without relying solely on your job. A side hustle allows you to make money outside of your 9-to-5 and can eventually grow into a significant source of income—or even replace your job entirely.

Here's a personal example: I began part-time real estate investing and financial planning in addition to my full-time work. What started as a small side business eventually became a reliable income stream, providing me the flexibility to save more, pay off debt, and diversify my income. I began researching real estate opportunities in my spare time, making small investments, and eventually helping others plan their finances. Over time, these ventures supplemented my income and became businesses I could grow and scale.

Here are some other side hustle ideas to consider:

1. **Freelancing**: If you have a skill—writing, graphic design, web development, or consulting—freelancing can be a lucrative side hustle. Websites like **Upwork**, **Fiverr**, and **Freelancer** offer platforms where you can connect with clients who need your services.

2. **Online Businesses**: The internet has made it easier than ever to start an online business. The possibilities are

endless, whether you're selling products through Etsy or Shopify, offering digital courses, or starting a blog or YouTube channel.
3. **Real Estate**: If you have some capital, investing in real estate—rental properties or Airbnb—can generate a steady stream of passive income.
4. **Gig Economy Jobs**: Platforms like **Uber**, **DoorDash**, and **TaskRabbit** offer flexible opportunities to earn extra money by driving, delivering, or helping people with tasks.

Step 3: Invest in Yourself – Boost Your Skills and Education

Investing in your skills and education is one of the best long-term strategies for increasing your income. The more valuable you are in the marketplace, the more you can earn. Whether learning a new skill, earning a certification, or pursuing further education, investing in yourself pays off.

Here's how to start:
1. **Identify High-Income Skills**: Focus on developing high-demand skills and command high salaries. These could include coding, data analysis, project management, sales, or marketing. Companies are willing to pay a premium for these skills.
2. **Take Online Courses**: There are countless online platforms like **Udemy**, **Coursera**, and **LinkedIn Learning** where you can learn new skills. Many of these courses are affordable and can be completed at your own pace.
3. **Network**: Building relationships with people in your industry or field can lead to new opportunities for higher-paying roles. Attend industry events, join professional organizations, and connect with others on LinkedIn to expand your network.
4. **Seek Mentorship**: Having a mentor who is already successful in your field can help you identify growth

areas and advise you on advancing your career. Look for mentors within your company or industry who can offer guidance and support.

Step 4: Diversify Your Income Streams

Relying on a single source of income can be risky. If you lose your job or experience a downturn in your industry, your financial stability could be at risk. That's why diversifying your income streams is one of the most innovative ways to increase economic security.

Here's how you can diversify:

1. **Invest in the Stock Market**: You can generate income through dividends and capital gains by investing in stocks, bonds, or index funds. As discussed in the investing chapter, start small and automate your contributions.
2. **Real Estate**: As mentioned earlier, real estate is a great way to create an additional income stream. Rental properties or real estate investments can provide passive income while appreciating over time.
3. **Create Digital Products**: If you have expertise in a particular area, consider creating digital products like e-books, online courses, or paid newsletters. Once created, these products can generate passive income, allowing you to earn money without ongoing work.

Step 5: Reinvest in Your Income Growth

Don't let lifestyle inflation consume your gains as you increase your income. One common mistake people make when earning more is spending more—on bigger homes, more excellent cars, or luxury items. Instead, reinvest part of your increased income into further growing your wealth.

Here's how:

- **Increase Your Savings Rate**: As your income grows,

increase the percentage of your income that goes toward savings and investments. This will help you build wealth faster.
- **Pay Down Debt Faster**: Use part of your increased income to accelerate debt repayment. The sooner you're debt-free, the more financial freedom you'll have.
- **Invest in Additional Income Streams**: Use your increased income to fund new income streams, whether through real estate, stocks, or business ventures.

Real-Life Example: How I Increased My Income Through Freelancing and Side Businesses

A few years ago, I realized I wanted to fast-track my financial goals, but my salary alone wasn't enough to get me there quickly. After work, I started freelancing in the evenings, offering writing services on platforms like Upwork. At the same time, I started exploring real estate investing on the side, and eventually, I ventured into financial planning for clients. At first, the extra income was small, but it grew steadily as I built my portfolio and took on more clients.

Eventually, my freelancing side hustle and real estate investing was generating enough income that I was able to invest more in the stock market, pay off debt faster, and even take a few vacations I wouldn't have been able to afford otherwise. The best part? The skills I gained through these ventures made me more valuable in my full-time job, leading to a promotion and a raise.

CONCLUSION: FOCUS ON GROWTH

Increasing your income is one of the most potent ways to build wealth and achieve your financial goals. Whether through negotiating a raise, starting a side hustle like I did with real estate and financial planning, or investing in your skills, the key is to focus on growth. The more income you generate, the more freedom you have to save, invest, and create the life you want.

Remember, there's no limit to how much you can earn, and by building multiple income streams, you'll create a more secure financial future. In the next chapter, we'll look at how to protect and grow your wealth through thoughtful financial planning and risk management.

PART 4: OVERCOMING CHALLENGES AND SETBACKS

Financial success is rarely a straight path. Life is full of changes, surprises, and setbacks, and your ability to adapt to these moments will determine your long-term financial health. Whether you're getting married, having children, retiring, or navigating an economic crisis, how you handle financial shifts is crucial to staying on course.

In this section, we'll explore how to adapt your financial habits when life throws you a curveball and how to create a sustainable, financially healthy lifestyle that can withstand change.

CHAPTER 9: ADAPTING TO FINANCIAL CHANGES

Life is full of changes—both planned and unexpected. From major milestones like getting married, having children, or retiring to unforeseen events like a health crisis or job loss, these transitions often bring significant shifts in your financial landscape. The key to maintaining financial health through these changes is adaptability. Just as you adjust to new circumstances in your personal life, your financial habits must evolve to meet the demands of each new chapter.

This chapter will explore how to modify your financial habits when life changes and examine case studies of individuals and families who successfully adapted their financial plans during crises. Whether the change is a joyful occasion or an unexpected challenge, handling your finances during these times will shape your long-term success.

Why Financial Adaptability Matters

Life doesn't follow a fixed plan, and neither should your finances. While having a solid financial foundation is essential, it's equally crucial to remain flexible. A budget that worked well for you when you were single might not be suitable when you're married with kids. The investment strategy that felt right in your 30s may need to shift as you approach retirement.

Being financially adaptable means being proactive about changing your habits to meet the demands of your current life stage. Instead of sticking to old systems that no longer serve you, adaptability allows you to optimize your financial decisions for each phase of life.

Here are some everyday life events that may require adjustments to your financial habits:

1. **Marriage**: Combining finances, setting joint financial goals, and managing shared expenses.
2. **Children**: Budgeting for new expenses like childcare, education, and healthcare while balancing long-term goals like college savings.
3. **Job Loss or Career Change**: Navigating periods of reduced income and adjusting savings and spending accordingly.
4. **Retirement**: Transitioning from regular paycheck to relying on savings, investments, and passive income streams.
5. **Health Crises**: Managing increased medical expenses and potential income disruptions.

Let's dive into how you can adapt your financial habits for each situation.

Adapting to Major Life Changes
1. Marriage: Combining Finances and Setting Joint Goals

Marriage brings more than just a union of hearts—it often involves combining finances. While this can be exciting, it's essential to approach it strategically. When you marry, you must consider merging your financial habits, setting joint goals, and navigating shared expenses.

Steps to Take:

- **Open the Conversation**: Have an open and honest conversation about your financial situation with your spouse. Discuss debts, income, savings, and spending habits. It's crucial to be transparent about money to

avoid future conflicts.
- **Set Joint Goals**: Whether buying a house, saving for travel, or planning for children, you must align your financial goals with your partner. Creating a shared vision for your future will make it easier to agree on how to manage your money.
- **Create a Joint Budget**: Some couples prefer to keep separate accounts, while others combine everything. Find a system that works for you, but create a joint budget that covers all household expenses, savings goals, and discretionary spending.

Case Study: *John and Sarah* When John and Sarah got married, they had very different spending habits—John was a saver, while Sarah loved to spend on experiences like dining out and traveling. To avoid conflict, they sat down together and created a joint budget to save for a home while setting aside a "fun money" fund for Sarah's travel desires. They could compromise without feeling restricted by aligning their financial goals and adjusting their habits.

---

2. Children: Managing New Expenses and Prioritizing Future Savings

The arrival of children brings immeasurable joy, but it also significantly increases expenses. Children can instantly change their financial priorities from diapers and daycare to college savings, and they modify their budget and savings strategy to account for these new costs.

Steps to Take:
- **Revisit Your Budget**: With the added expenses of children, your budget will need a complete overhaul. Factor in childcare, healthcare, and education costs, and reduce discretionary spending to balance your budget.
- **Start College Savings Early**: College might seem far away when your child is born, but the sooner you start saving, the better. Consider setting up a 529 plan or other education savings account.
- **Increase Your Emergency Fund**: With kids in the picture, it's even more important to have a robust

emergency fund to cover unexpected expenses like medical bills or unforeseen events.

Case Study: *Emily and David* When Emily and David welcomed their first child, they quickly realized how much their budget had to change. They cut back on non-essential spending, sold one of their cars to reduce costs, and set up a 529 plan to start saving for their child's education. By being proactive about their finances, they were able to balance the new costs of parenthood while continuing to work toward their long-term goals.

---

3. Job Loss or Career Change: Navigating Reduced Income

Losing a job or changing careers can disrupt your financial stability, especially if it leads to a temporary reduction in income. During these times, it's crucial to reassess your financial habits, reduce spending, and focus on preserving your savings until you regain economic stability.

Steps to Take:
- **Reduce Discretionary Spending**: Immediately cut back on non-essential expenses like dining out, entertainment, and luxury purchases. Focus only on necessary expenses such as rent, groceries, and utilities.
- **Use Your Emergency Fund Wisely**: If you have an emergency fund, this is the time to use it. Be mindful, though, and limit withdrawals to essential expenses to make your savings last as long as possible.
- **Look for Temporary Income**: Consider taking on freelance work, part-time jobs, or side hustles to bring in additional income between jobs. This can help offset some of the financial strain.

Case Study: *Michael* When Michael lost his job during an economic downturn, he quickly pivoted to freelance work to cover his essential expenses. He slashed his non-essential spending, including canceling his gym membership and eating out less. By focusing on temporary work and reducing his costs, Michael avoided dipping too deeply into his emergency fund while he searched for a new full-time job.

4. Retirement: Shifting from Earning to Living Off Savings

Retirement is a time of transition from earning a regular paycheck to relying on your savings, investments, and passive income. As you approach retirement, your financial habits must shift to ensure your money lasts through your golden years.

Steps to Take:

- **Create a Retirement Budget**: Your retirement budget should reflect your new income sources—such as Social Security, pensions, and retirement savings withdrawals. Plan for healthcare costs, travel, and other retirement activities while ensuring your money lasts.
- **Review Your Investments**: As you approach retirement, it may be time to adjust your investment portfolio to be more conservative, reducing exposure to high-risk assets while focusing on preserving capital.
- **Plan for Healthcare Costs**: Healthcare is one of the most significant expenses in retirement. Ensure you have adequate insurance coverage, including Medicare, and consider setting up a Health Savings Account (HSA) if you're still eligible.

Case Study: *Laura* When Laura retired, she realized she needed to adjust her lifestyle to align with her new fixed income. She downsized her home to reduce expenses, moved to a state with lower taxes, and focused on making the most of her retirement savings. By staying mindful of her budget and prioritizing her long-term financial health, Laura could enjoy her retirement without financial stress.

Adapting Financial Plans During Crises

Sometimes, life throws unexpected challenges—a health crisis, divorce, or global recession. These situations require fast action and financial flexibility to navigate the uncertainty successfully.

Steps to Take:

- **Cut Non-Essentials Quickly**: When facing a financial crisis, it's essential to reduce unnecessary expenses immediately. Focus on preserving cash for critical needs.

- **Reach Out for Support**: Financial assistance may be available through insurance, government programs, or charitable organizations in cases of health crises or unexpected hardship. Don't hesitate to seek help when needed.
- **Reassess Your Goals**: During crises, long-term financial goals might need to be prioritized over short-term survival. Prioritize the immediate need for cash flow and economic stability, and revisit your long-term goals once the crisis subsides.

CONCLUSION: EMBRACE FINANCIAL FLEXIBILITY

Life changes are inevitable, but how you handle your finances during these transitions can determine your long-term success. You can confidently navigate any life event by staying adaptable, regularly reassessing your financial goals and adjusting your habits to meet new challenges.

In the next chapter, we'll discuss creating a **financially healthy lifestyle**, incorporating all the habits we've covered into a cohesive, long-term plan. With the right strategies, you can maintain your financial health through life's ups and downs.

CHAPTER 10: CREATING A FINANCIALLY HEALTHY LIFESTYLE

There's a moment, maybe late at night, when the house is quiet or during a long walk when you pause and wonder: *Is this the life I want?* It's a question I've asked myself more times than I can count, especially when I was buried under a mountain of financial decisions. I used to think that once my finances were "under control," everything else would fall into place. But I quickly realized that economic health isn't just about hitting savings goals or eliminating debt—it's about building a life that feels rich in every sense. A life where money isn't a source of stress but a tool that helps you live freely and fully.

Have you ever thought about what financial freedom looks like for you? It's different for everyone. For some, it's the ability to travel whenever they want; for others, it's knowing they can care for their family without financial worry. It was about feeling secure enough to make choices aligned with my values—prioritizing experiences over material things, investing in relationships, and having the space to pursue passions without worrying about money.

This chapter brings everything together—all the habits, lessons, and strategies you've learned—and turns them into a lifestyle. A financially healthy lifestyle isn't about sacrifice; it's about balance, intention, and living in a way that supports your goals while allowing you to enjoy the present moment. Let's explore how you can weave these financial habits into a life that feels abundant, fulfilling, and aligned with your values.

The Journey to Balance: Redefining Wealth

There was a time when I thought wealth meant having a specific number in my bank account or checking off a list of financial goals. I felt that if I could reach that next milestone—pay off that credit card, max out my retirement account, or save for a house—I'd finally feel secure. But as I reached those goals, I realized something was missing.

One evening, after a particularly grueling week, I sat down and asked myself, *What's all this for?* I had been so focused on saving and hitting the financial targets that I'd forgotten to enjoy the life I was working so hard to build. I was saving for the future, but I wasn't living fully in the present.

That night, I made a decision. I wouldn't wait for some distant future to enjoy my life. I was going to find a balance where I could save and invest for my future and create space for joy, experiences, and connection right now. That's when I started to redefine what wealth meant to me. Wealth, I realized, isn't just about money. It's about freedom. It's about having choices. It's about feeling secure enough to live in alignment with my values.

So, let me ask you: What does wealth mean to you? Please take a moment to think about it. Is it about financial security, the ability to travel, or maybe just the peace of mind that comes from knowing you're in control of your money, not the other way around? Whatever it is, let that definition guide you as you create your own financially healthy lifestyle.

Bringing All Your Financial Habits Together

You've worked hard to develop habits that support your financial goals—tracking your spending, budgeting, saving, investing, and managing debt. But now it's time to bring all of those habits together into a cohesive system that doesn't just serve your financial needs but also supports the life you want to live.

Think of these habits as tools in your financial toolkit. Each habit has its purpose, but it creates something powerful when used together. *Imagine your financial habits as the threads of a tapestry. Each thread might seem insignificant, but when woven together, they make a picture of a stable, abundant, and free life.*

Here's how you can start weaving your financial habits into a system that supports your life:

1. **Track Your Progress with Gratitude**
    Tracking your spending and monitoring your budget isn't just about numbers—it's about reflecting on what those numbers represent. Every time you check your finances, pause and ask yourself: *How is this helping me live a more aligned life?* Maybe your budget allowed you to save for a trip with friends or invest in a course that expanded your skills. Celebrate these moments of alignment, and express gratitude for your progress. Connecting your financial habits to a sense of purpose will make them feel less like chores and more like steps toward a life you love.

2. **Automate for Freedom, Not Just Convenience**
    We've talked about automation to streamline your savings, bill payments, and investments. But automation isn't just about convenience—it's about creating freedom. When you automate your finances, you free up mental space to focus on what matters to you. Your money works for you in the background, quietly building wealth while you live your life. It's like planting and watching a garden grow, knowing you've set it up to flourish without constant oversight. Let automation be your foundation so you can spend more time living and less time worrying.

3. **Celebrate the Journey, Not Just the Destination**
   One of the most powerful shifts you can make is learning to celebrate the small wins along the way. It's easy to focus on the big goals—buying a house, paying off debt, reaching financial independence—but the journey is just as important. Maybe you made your first investment or paid off a credit card. These moments are worth celebrating. Treat yourself to something small—perhaps a favorite meal or a quiet afternoon doing something you love. These celebrations create momentum and remind you that progress is worth acknowledging, no matter how small.

Adapting to Life's Unpredictable Moments

Here's something I've learned the hard way: life rarely goes according to plan. There will be times when everything seems to be going smoothly—your budget is in order, your savings are growing—and then, out of nowhere, life throws you a curveball. Maybe it's a job loss, an unexpected medical bill, or a global pandemic that disrupts everything.

I've been there. I remember the time when a sudden health crisis left me with medical bills I hadn't planned for. I had been diligent with my savings, but the costs were overwhelming. For a while, I felt defeated—like all the progress I had made was slipping away. But it was during that time that I learned one of the most valuable lessons: *resilience isn't about avoiding setbacks; it's about how you respond to them.*

Resilience is your greatest asset when life doesn't go as planned. It's the ability to adjust, pivot, and keep moving forward, even when things feel uncertain. When faced with financial challenges, allow yourself to pause, reassess, and make adjustments. Maybe you need to scale back your savings for a few months or find new ways to generate income. The key is to stay adaptable and remind yourself that setbacks are temporary, but your commitment to your financial health is long-term.

Reflection Exercise: Discovering Your "Why"

One of the most potent motivators for financial health is knowing your "why." Why does this matter to you? Why are you working so hard to build a financially healthy lifestyle? Take a moment right now to reflect on your deeper "why." Is it the freedom to travel, the security of knowing you can care for your family, or the ability to pursue your passions without financial worry?

Once you've identified your "why," write it down and keep it somewhere you'll often see—a note on your phone, a sticky note on your desk, or even as the background on your computer. Let it be your anchor, guiding you through tough decisions and reminding you of what's truly important.

Creating a Financially Healthy Lifestyle That Lasts

Building a financially healthy lifestyle is a journey, not a destination. It's not about hitting a certain number in your bank account or reaching a specific goal—it's about cultivating habits and a mindset that will serve you for the rest of your life. This means staying flexible, open to change, and committed to growth.

As your life evolves, so too will your financial needs and goals. Maybe you'll get married, have children, change careers, or retire early. Each of these life stages will require you to adapt your financial habits. The important thing is to stay grounded in your values, reassess your goals regularly, and keep moving forward—no matter what life throws your way.

Conclusion: Embrace Financial Freedom as a Journey

As we wrap up this chapter and this book, I want to leave you with one final thought: **financial health isn't about perfection.** It's about progress. It's about taking small, consistent steps toward the life you want to create. It's about finding balance—between enjoying life now and planning for the future, between being disciplined and allowing yourself room for joy.

The journey to financial freedom and fulfillment is ongoing. There will be moments of triumph, setbacks, and deep reflection. But through it all, remember that you have the tools, knowledge, and resilience to create a rich, abundant life that aligns with your values.

So here's to your journey. May it be filled with growth, joy, and financial peace today and in the future.

Reflecting on everything you've learned, one thing becomes clear: **solid financial habits are the foundation of a life well-lived**. These habits—tracking your spending, budgeting, saving, investing, and managing debt—aren't just tasks to check off a list. They are practices that empower you to build the life you want, one decision at a time.

We've explored the journey of creating a healthy lifestyle, from cultivating balance in spending and saving to adapting your finances when life changes unexpectedly. The key has been consistency, mindfulness, and the courage to embrace the present and the future.

But this is only the beginning. **Financial growth is a journey**, not a destination. It's a path you'll walk for the rest of your life, evolving with you as your goals and circumstances change. There will be moments of success and moments of challenge, but with the habits you've built, you're equipped to handle it all.

Start small, think big. Whether you're just beginning your financial journey or looking to refine your habits, remember that progress is made in small, consistent steps. It's not about getting everything perfect immediately—it's about committing to the process and trusting that every step you take moves you closer to your financial goals.

CALL TO ACTION

As you close this book, I encourage you to take action. Start with a tiny habit today. Maybe it's setting up a budget, automating your savings, or tracking your spending for the first time. **Small actions compound over time**, leading to significant financial growth.

You don't have to have it all figured out right now. Just take the next step. Trust yourself, trust the process, and know you're building a future that aligns with your deepest values and desires.

Here's to your financial journey. May it be filled with progress, abundance, and the freedom to live the life you've always dreamed of.

www.ingramcontent.com/pod-product-compliance
Lightning Source LLC
Chambersburg PA
CBHW070401230526
45471CB00006B/2659